Univers;

# HUMAN
# RIGHTS

Proclaimed by the
United Nations General Assembly
Paris, December 1948

BODLEIAN
LIBRARY
PUBLISHING

# Foreword

There are few historical developments more significant than the realization that those in power should not be free to torture and abuse those who are not. The Universal Declaration of Human Rights, adopted in the aftermath of genocide by the Nazis, described limits on the power of the state by defining the human rights that every individual is entitled to by virtue of being human. As French jurist René Cassin, one of the Universal Declaration's framers, argued: 'we do not want a repetition of what happened in 1933, where Germany began to massacre its own nationals, and everybody ... bowed, saying "Thou art sovereign and master in thine own house"'.

The Universal Declaration is the centrepiece of the modern human rights infrastructure set up following the Second World War. It was adopted a day after the Genocide Convention, within months of the Geneva Conventions, and while the Nuremberg trials of Nazi leaders were ongoing. It was quite a feat to obtain consensus from the fifty-eight nations that then formed the United Nations on a list of universal rights. And when Eleanor Roosevelt presented it to the UN General Assembly she did so with the ambition that it would become the 'Magna Carta' for all of mankind.

The Declaration is, today, considered the most widely cited human rights instrument, and it has been translated into over 500 languages. Its preamble considers human rights to be the 'foundation of freedom, justice and peace', the primary purposes of the United Nations. Its rationale is derived not from religion but the idea that since an individual comes into the world through no fault of his or her own, he or she is a member of the 'human family' entitled to certain inalienable rights. It describes fundamental freedoms from torture and slavery and prerequisites for democracy like the right to free speech, protest, and fair trial. Two decades later, its key promises were defined in the International Covenant on Civil and Political Rights, which has now been ratified by 173 of the world's 195 nations, and in a similar treaty on economic, social and cultural rights.

The Declaration's goals are as relevant today as when they were first adopted a lifetime ago, and their attainment remains elusive and urgent. Women are still denied equal treatment, a scourge that holds back half the population in countries across the globe. Journalists are put behind bars for simply reporting the truth. Survivors of genocide like the Yazidis and the Rohingya still await a judicial reckoning.

Having defined universal rights, states must do more to make sure they are enforced. The Declaration was meant to prevent the repetition of 'barbarous acts' that 'outraged the conscience of mankind' – but this cannot happen unless violators are punished for such acts. That means that, just like the Nazi leaders who were held accountable for their crimes at Nuremberg, human rights abusers today must face justice for their crimes.

Soviet Foreign Minister Andrei Vyshinsky described the Universal Declaration at the time it was adopted as 'just a collection of pious phrases'. There are few objectives more worthwhile than proving him wrong. And we all have a part to play. As one of the Declaration's drafters, Eleanor Roosevelt, said:

"Where, after all, do universal human rights begin? In small places, close to home ... [W]ithout concerned citizen action to uphold them close to home, we shall look in vain for progress in the larger world".

Amal Clooney

# Introduction

The Universal Declaration of Human Rights
was adopted by the United Nations General
Assembly in 1948, and is customarily seen as
a response to the horrors of the Second World
War and a determination not to repeat them. In
this interpretation, its genesis can be seen in US
President Franklin D. Roosevelt's 1941 State of the
Union address, in which he called for the protection
of what he termed the 'Four Freedoms': the freedom
of speech and expression, the freedom of worship,
the freedom from want and the freedom from fear.
This was followed by the Atlantic Charter, signed by
Roosevelt and Winston Churchill at their meeting at
sea on 14 June 1941, whose stated aims included a
determination to work towards achieving the third
and fourth of Roosevelt's Four Freedoms, as well
as the freedom of self-determination for nations,
and in January 1942 by the Declaration of the United
Nations which explicitly referred to human rights.

At the same time, many non-governmental organizations and associations also began to press for human rights to be included as part of any eventual peace treaty at the end of the war. For example, in early 1943 the American Institute of Law produced a draft for an International Bill of Rights, and this was followed by a similar document compiled by the International Labour Organization. Churches too were active in calling for the rights of the oppressed or minority groups to be recognized in any peace settlement, with 750,000 copies of a pamphlet compiled jointly by Protestant, Catholic and Jewish leaders in the United States and called *A Pattern for Peace* being distributed in 1943. This title was taken up by churches and religious groups elsewhere. In Australia, for example, the Catholic church published a similar programme, which aimed to 'give a definite status to every man and woman in Australia'.

However, the event which had the greatest immediate influence on the drafting and subsequent adoption of the Declaration of Human Rights was probably the Inter-American Conference on War and Peace, which took place in Mexico City in February and March 1945. Here, twenty-one American countries agreed that they wanted to see a declaration of human rights as part of the Charter of the United Nations Organization, then in process of formation, and three of them – Cuba, Chile and Panama – were the first nations to submit a draft of such a bill. This was later acknowledged by members of the Drafting Committee to be one of 'the best of the texts' from which they worked when drawing up the Declaration.

But if these were its immediate origins, it is nevertheless true that the Declaration can also be seen, if not as the culmination, then at least as a very significant milestone in a much longer history of the acceptance of certain basic human rights worldwide. Indeed, the first known use of the term 'human rights' has been attributed to Tertullian, who, in his letter to Scapula (*c.*212 CE), wrote that 'it is a fundamental human right, a privilege of nature, that every man should worship according to his own convictions'. However, in the Western world, the foundations of modern human rights lie more directly in the Renaissance and the period of the Enlightenment.

Key documents from this period which unquestionably influenced those who drafted the Declaration include the English Bill of Rights (1689), with its provision protecting individuals from cruel and unusual punishment, the American Declaration of Independence (1776) and Bill of Rights (1791), and the French Declaration of the Rights of Man and of the Citizen (1789). However, it should be noted that none of these documents were universal in their application, significant sections of society, including women, slaves, and those who were defined in various ways as non- or passive citizens, being regularly excluded.

Human rights first formed part of a multilateral treaty at the Congress of Vienna (1814–15) following the end of the Napoleonic wars, where, largely as a result of British pressure, the leading European powers – Austria, Britain, Prussia, Russia, France, Portugal, Spain and Sweden – agreed the Declaration of the Eight Courts Relative to the Universal Abolition of the Slave Trade on 8 February 1815. This condemned the slave trade as 'repugnant to the principles of humanity and universal morality', and the text was subsequently incorporated into the

Final Act of the Congress as Annex XV. Although the Declaration was principally aspirational, and did not impose any immediate practical obligations on the signatories, it nevertheless introduced the abolition of the slave trade as a general principle into international law, and became a point of reference for anti-slavery campaigners throughout the nineteenth century.

The League of Nations, established after the carnage of the First World War, saw itself as primarily an arbiter of disputes between states, but it is worth noting that human rights were directly addressed in Article 23 of its Covenant which stated that members of the League would:

> endeavour to secure and maintain fair and humane conditions of labour for men, women and children … and for that purpose will establish and maintain the necessary international <u>organisations</u>.
>
> undertake to ensure just treatment of the native inhabitants of territories under their control.

entrust the League with the general supervision over the execution of agreements with regard to the traffic in women and children.

Subsequently, largely as a result of pressure from Eglantyne Jebb, the founder of Save the Children, the League adopted their Declaration of the Rights of the Child in 1924. It also, in the same year, established a temporary Slavery Commission, whose work led to the 1926 Convention to Suppress the Slave Trade and Slavery, which, in an amended form, still exists today.

At the San Francisco Conference (April–June 1945), which formally established the United Nations Organization, a Commission on Human Rights was established, one of whose tasks was to write an international bill of rights. In his closing speech to the conference, President Harry Truman made this explicit when he said that 'we have good reason to expect the framing of an international bill of rights [which] will be as much part of international life as our own Bill of Rights is a part of our Constitution'.[1] Work on drafting what became the Universal Declaration of Human Rights began in January

1947, when the first session of the Human Rights Commission was held.

The chairperson of the Commission, and of the committee to which it delegated the task of drafting the Universal Declaration, was Eleanor Roosevelt (1884–1962), the former First Lady of the United States from 1933 to 1945. With a strong track record of support both for the civil rights movement in the United States and for refugees during the war, she was an ideal choice for the position, and her high profile and credibility with both superpowers enabled her to steer the drafting process to a successful conclusion. In 1968 she was posthumously awarded the UN Human Rights Prize.

Her colleagues on the drafting committee were drawn from a variety of backgrounds and included representatives from each of the major victorious powers at the end of the war:

**JOHN PETERS HUMPHREY** (1905–1995) was a Canadian academic lawyer, specializing in international law. In 1946 he was appointed as the first Director of the United Nations Division of

Human Rights. As the lead official on the Drafting Committee he was responsible for gathering and analysing the background documents which informed the Committee's work. However, his true input was far greater than this. His 408-page 'Documented Outline' was in effect the first draft of the Declaration, and was notable for its inclusivity. In spite of the many discussions which followed and the hundreds of amendments which were put forward, Humphrey's draft remained the core around which the rest of the document was created, and he has a good claim to be regarded as its principal, although by no means its only, author.

Fluent in both English and French, and with a wide range of academic interests, Humphrey also acted as bridge between other members of the committee, scholars and pragmatists, politicians and civil servants. His guiding philosophy, as expressed in a letter to his sister many years before, can perhaps be applied to all those who worked to create the Declaration in a remarkably short period of time: 'It's the good a chap can do for the good of humanity ... that counts, not the good that he does for himself'.[2]

He remained working with the United Nations for the next twenty years until returning to academic life in Canada, and in 1988 he was awarded the UN Human Rights Prize. In 2008 a memorial to him commemorating his key role in the drafting of the Declaration was unveiled in his home town of Hampton, New Brunswick.

**RENÉ CASSIN** (1887–1976) was a French jurist whose involvement in the drafting of the Declaration, as well as his other human rights work, was influenced to significant degree by his personal response to the Holocaust. Through his work at the League of Nations between 1924 and 1938, he showed his commitment to disarmament and the use of international institutions for conflict resolution.

Following the Second World War, during which he served as a member of the Free French government in exile in London, he was assigned to the United Nations, where he played an important part in the drafting of the Declaration of Human Rights. Working from the first draft of John Humphrey, he created the document's structure, incorporating a preamble and certain basic principles.

Cassin later became a member (1959–65) and president (1965–68) of the European Court of Human Rights, and he was awarded the Nobel Peace Prize in 1968.

**CHARLES HABIB MALIK** (1906–1987) was a Lebanese academic, philosopher and diplomat. He represented Lebanon at the San Francisco conference at which the United Nations was founded, He was *Rapporteur* for the Human Rights Commission, and, along with Peng-chun Chang played an important role in explaining and refining some of the basic conceptual issues to other less philosophically minded members of the committee.

Malik subsequently served as Lebanese Minister of Education and Fine Arts (1956–57) and Minister of Foreign Affairs (1956–58), as well as resuming his academic career. After the outbreak of the Lebanese Civil War in 1975 he founded the Front for Freedom and Man in Lebanon.

**PENG-CHUN CHANG** (1892–1957) was the Vice-Chair of the Human Rights Commission. He was a playwright, philosopher and educator, who had studied in the United States and taught at Nankai University in Tianjin.

Chang shared with Charles Malik the ideal of universal human rights, but disagreed with him as to how these could best be described in an international document. John Humphrey thought that the two hated each other, but they were also the two who led the discussions at the philosophical level. Chang insisted, in the name of universalism, on the removal of all allusions to nature and God from the text of the Declaration.

**HERNÁN SANTA CRUZ** (1906–1999) was a Chilean lawyer who was appointed as Chile's Permanent Representative to the United Nations in 1946. On the drafting committee he held no particular position, but John Humphrey later recorded that his contribution to its work was a significant one. He had supplied Humphrey with some of the initial drafts and took an especial interest in the provisions relating to socio-economic rights, successfully arguing that they were inseparable from political and civil rights. It has subsequently been said of him that he was responsible for the shift in the text away from eighteenth-century Enlightenment philosophy towards a wider and more modern definition of human rights.[3]

**WILLIAM HODGSON** (1892–1958) was an Australian career soldier, who was seriously wounded at Gallipoli (he survived to read his own obituary). In 1935 he was appointed secretary of the newly created Department of External Affairs, and from 1945 to 1957 he served overseas, carrying out a wide variety of functions at international conferences and on international commissions. In this capacity he was the Australian delegate to the first General Assembly, held in London in 1945–46, before becoming Australia's representative on both the Security Council and the Human Rights Commission. He advocated the establishment of both a multilateral convention on human rights and an international court to implement and enforce it.

Hodgson had the reputation of being something of a martinet, who could be blunt and rather aggressive when dealing with others – his voice was reported to have been 'like a cross-cut saw' – but in his work for the UN his 'practical and common-sense approach to problems' was said to have made 'a very real impact'.[4]

The Soviet Union was represented by **ALEXANDER BOGOMOLOV** (1900–1969), a career diplomat who was regarded as one of Molotov's closest advisors. Harold Macmillan, who came to know him during the Second World War, regarded him as 'naturally shifty' and the kind of man who would slowly poison one in 'indifferent French wine'.[5] He had spent his early career in the military, and had also been a professor of dialectical and historical materialism at Moscow State University. From 1940 to 1941 he served as the Soviet ambassador to Vichy France, before moving to London to become ambassador to the allied governments in exile, towards whom he was said to display a 'truculent' and bullying attitude.[6]

Bogomolov was later the Soviet delegate to the 1948 Geneva conference on freedom of information and the press. When accused of coming from a country which had neither, he responded by accusing the British and American press of being under 'a censorship of dollars and sterling'.[7] After serving as Soviet ambassador to Czechoslovakia and Italy, he retired in 1957.

The British representative on the committee was **CHARLES DUKES**, later **LORD DUKESTON** (1881–1948), a trade unionist and Labour Party politician who had served as MP for Warrington (1923–24 and 1929–31), and as General Secretary of the National Union of General and Municipal Workers (1934–46). His appointment seems to have been based on his being a 'crony' of the British Foreign Secretary, Ernie Bevin. This resulted in his fitness for the appointment being questioned in the House of Commons on the grounds that, as a trade unionist, he was in favour of the closed shop; in reply, the Foreign Office minister Hector McNeil said that 'there is probably no institution in the world other than the British trade union which has taken such an interest in [human rights]'.

Humphrey disliked Dukes and thought he was lukewarm over the protection of human rights. However, a recent study suggests that he was far more in favour of them than the British Foreign Office of the time, and often went against his instructions from London. His general line was that, as he himself said, he 'did not think there could be unrestricted individual liberty in any modern community', but that the key lay in the right to freedom of association combined with 'the co-existence and closely knit interdependence of the State and the individual'.[8]

Dukes returned from Geneva at the end of 1947 suffering from a septic lung condition, and died the following May.

However, to focus entirely on the members of the official drafting committee is to downplay the input from other members of the Commission, some of whom played a major role in the process. To take a few examples:

**HANSA MEHTA** (1897–1995), the Indian delegate, was a prominent educationalist and campaigner for women's rights, who had played a prominent role in the  struggle for Indian independence. In 1946, as president of the All-India Women's Conference, she had proposed and drafted the Indian Woman's Charter of Rights and Duties, which, amongst other things, called for equal pay and the equal application of marriage laws. It was largely at her urging that the text of article 1 of the Declaration was changed from 'All men are born free and equal' (as proposed by Eleanor Roosevelt) to 'All human beings are born free and equal', highlighting the need for gender equality.[9]

**BEGUM SHAISTA IKRAMULLAH** (1915–2000) of Pakistan was a distinguished author and diplomat who championed the inclusion of article 16, on equal rights in marriage, which she saw as a way of combatting child marriage and forced marriage.[10]

**CARLOS ROMULO** (1898–1985), from the Philippines, argued that full rights should be given to those subject to colonial rule, leading to the inclusion of the final sentence of article 2, which states that  'no distinction shall be made on the basis of the political, jurisdictional or international status of the country or territory to which a person belongs, whether it be independent, trust, non-self-governing or under any other limitation of sovereignty'.

By its resolution 217 A (III) of 10 December 1948, the General Assembly, meeting at the Palais de Chaillot in Paris, adopted the Universal Declaration of Human Rights. Forty-eight of the fifty-eight nations then comprising the United Nations voted in favour. None voted against but there were eight abstentions, these being the Byelorussian SSR, Czechoslovakia, Poland, Saudi Arabia, South Africa, the Soviet Union, the Ukrainian SSR and Yugoslavia; in addition the representatives of Honduras and Yemen, although present, refrained from voting without formally recording their abstention.

Hernán Santa Cruz wrote of the occasion:

> I perceived clearly that I was participating in a truly significant historic event in which a consensus had been reached as to the supreme value of the human person, a value that did not

originate in the decision of a worldly power, but rather in the fact of existing – which gave rise to the inalienable right to live free from want and oppression and to fully develop one's personality. In the Great Hall … there was an atmosphere of genuine solidarity and brotherhood among men and women from all latitudes, the like of which I have not seen again in any international setting.

More pithily, Eleanor Roosevelt called the Declaration 'the international Magna Carta' for everyone, everywhere.

John Pinfold

# FURTHER READING

R. Cassin, *La Déclaration universelle des droits de l'homme de 1948* (Paris: Institut de France, Académie des Sciences Morales et Politiques, 1958). This essay also appears in R. Cassin, *La Pensée et l'action* (Paris: Lalou, 1972)

M.A. Glendon, *A World Made New: Eleanor Roosevelt and the Universal Declaration of Human Rights* (New York: Random House, 2001)

A.J. Hobbins, ed., *On the Edge of Greatness: The Diaries of John Humphrey, First Director of the United Nations Division of Human Rights* (Montreal: McGill University Press, 1984)

J.P. Humphrey, *Human Rights and the United Nations: A Great Adventure* (Dobbs Ferry, NY: Transnational, 1984)

H. Malik, *The Challenge of Human Rights: Charles Malik and the Universal Declaration* (Oxford: Charles Malik Foundation, 2000)

J. Morsink, *The Universal Declaration of Human Rights: Origins, Drafting, and Intent* (Philadelphia: University of Pennsylvania Press, 1999)

A.W.B. Simpson, *Human Rights and the End of Empire* (Oxford: Oxford University Press, 2001)

S. Waltz, 'Universalizing Human Rights: The Role of Small States in the Construction of the Universal Declaration of Human Rights', *Human Rights Quarterly*, 23 (2001), pp. 44–72

# NOTES

1 H.S. Truman, *Year of Decisions* (Garden City, NY: Doubleday, 1955), p.292.

2 Quoted in J. Morsink, *The Universal Declaration of Human Rights: Origins, Drafting, and Intent* (Philadelphia: University of Pennsylvania Press, 1999), p.133.

3 S. Waltz, 'Universalizing Human Rights: The Role of Small States in the Construction of the Universal Declaration of Human Rights', *Human Rights Quarterly*, 23 (2001), p.60.

4 A. Watt, 'Hodgson, William Roy' in the *Australian Dictionary of National Biography* (Melbourne: Melbourne University Press, 1983), vol. 9; available online at: http://adb.anu.edu.au/biography/hodgson-william-roy-6695 (accessed 7 December 2020); *The Courier-Mail* (Brisbane), 26 April 1946; *Canberra Times*, 25 January 1958.

5 A. Horne, *Macmillan 1894–1956* (London: Macmillan, 1988), p.203.

6 M.H. Folly, 'British Attempts to Forge a Political Partnership with the Kremlin, 1942–3', *Journal of Contemporary History*, 53 (1) (2018), p.192.

7 *Daily Herald*, 31 March 1948.

8 For Dukes and the British government's policy towards the Human Rights Commission see A.W.B. Simpson, *Human Rights and the End of Empire* (Oxford: Oxford University Press, 2001), especially pp.351–77.

9 https://www.livehistoryindia.com/herstory/2020/07/09/hansa-mehta (accessed 7 December 2020).

10 *The Express Tribune*, 24 November 2018.

# Universal Declaration of
# Human Rights

## PREAMBLE

WHEREAS recognition of the inherent dignity and of the equal and inalienable rights of all members of the human family is the foundation of freedom, justice and peace in the world,

WHEREAS disregard and contempt for human rights have resulted in barbarous acts which have outraged the conscience of mankind, and the advent of a world in which human beings shall enjoy freedom of speech and belief and freedom from fear and want has been proclaimed as the highest aspiration of the common people,

WHEREAS it is essential, if man is not to be compelled to have recourse, as a last resort, to rebellion against tyranny and oppression, that human rights should be protected by the rule of law,

WHEREAS it is essential to promote the development of friendly relations between nations,

WHEREAS the peoples of the United Nations have in the Charter reaffirmed their faith in fundamental human rights, in the dignity and worth of the human person and in the equal rights of men and women and have determined to promote social progress and better standards of life in larger freedom,

WHEREAS Member States have pledged themselves to achieve, in co-operation with the United Nations, the promotion of universal respect for and observance of human rights and fundamental freedoms,

WHEREAS a common understanding of these rights and freedoms is of the greatest importance for the full realization of this pledge,

Now, therefore,
THE GENERAL ASSEMBLY
Proclaims THIS UNIVERSAL DECLARATION
OF HUMAN RIGHTS as a common standard of
achievement for all peoples and all nations, to the
end that every individual and every organ of society,
keeping this Declaration constantly in mind, shall
strive by teaching and education to promote respect
for these rights and freedoms and by progressive
measures, national and international, to secure their
universal and effective recognition and observance,
both among the peoples of Member States themselves and among the peoples of territories under
their jurisdiction.

Article

All human beings are born free and equal in dignity and rights. They are endowed with reason and conscience and should act towards one another in a spirit of brotherhood.

Article **2**

Everyone is entitled to all the rights and freedoms set forth in this Declaration, without distinction of any kind, such as race, colour, sex, language, religion, political or other opinion, national or social origin, property, birth or other status. Furthermore, no distinction shall be made on the basis of the political, jurisdictional or international status of the country or territory to which a person belongs, whether it be independent, trust, non-self-governing or under any other limitation of sovereignty.

Article 3

Everyone has the right to life, liberty and security of person.

Article 4

No one shall be held in slavery or servitude; slavery and the slave trade shall be prohibited in all their forms.

No one shall be subjected to torture
or to cruel, inhuman or degrading
treatment or punishment.

Article **6**

Everyone has the right
to recognition everywhere
as a person before the law.

Article

All are equal before the law and are entitled without any discrimination to equal protection of the law. All are entitled to equal protection against any discrimination in violation of this Declaration and against any incitement to such discrimination.

# Article 8

Everyone has the right to an effective remedy by the competent national tribunals for acts violating the fundamental rights granted him by the constitution or by law.

Article

No one shall be subjected to
arbitrary arrest, detention or exile.

Article **10**

Everyone is entitled in full equality
to a fair and public hearing by
an independent and impartial
tribunal, in the determination of his
rights and obligations and
of any criminal charge against him.

Article **11**

## 1

Everyone charged with a penal offence has the right to be presumed innocent until proved guilty according to law in a public trial at which he has had all the guarantees necessary for his defence.

## 2

No one shall be held guilty of any penal offence on account of any act or omission which did not constitute a penal offence, under national or international law, at the time when it was committed. Nor shall a heavier penalty be imposed than the one that was applicable at the time the penal offence was committed.

Article **12**

No one shall be subjected to arbitrary interference with his privacy, family, home or correspondence, nor to attacks upon his honour and reputation. Everyone has the right to the protection of the law against such interference or attacks.

Article **13**

## 1

Everyone has the right to freedom of movement and residence within the borders of each State.

## 2

Everyone has the right to leave any country, including his own, and to return to his country.

# Article **14**

# 1

Everyone has the right to seek and to enjoy in other countries asylum from persecution.

# 2

This right may not be invoked in the case of prosecutions genuinely arising from non-political crimes or from acts contrary to the purposes and principles of the United Nations.

Article **15**

**1**

Everyone has the right to a nationality.

**2**

No one shall be arbitrarily deprived of his nationality nor denied the right to change his nationality.

Article **16**

## 1

Men and women of full age, without any limitation due to race, nationality or religion, have the right to marry and to found a family. They are entitled to equal rights as to marriage, during marriage and at its dissolution.

## 2

Marriage shall be entered into only with the free and full consent of the intending spouses.

## 3

The family is the natural and fundamental group unit of society and is entitled to protection by society and the State.

Article **17**

## 1

Everyone has the right to own property alone
as well as in association with others.

## 2

No one shall be arbitrarily deprived of his
property.

Article **18**

Everyone has the right to freedom
of thought, conscience and religion;
this right includes freedom to change
his religion or belief, and freedom,
either alone or in community with
others and in public or private, to
manifest his religion or belief
in teaching, practice, worship
and observance.

Article **19**

Everyone has the right to freedom of opinion and expression; this right includes freedom to hold opinions without interference and to seek, receive and impart information and ideas through any media and regardless of frontiers.

Article **20**

## 1

Everyone has the right to freedom
of peaceful assembly and
association.

## 2

No one may be compelled to
belong to an association.

# Article 21

# 1

Everyone has the right to take part in the government of his country, directly or through freely chosen representatives.

# 2

Everyone has the right of equal access to public service in his country.

# 3

The will of the people shall be the basis of the authority of government; this will shall be expressed in periodic and genuine elections which shall be by universal and equal suffrage and shall be held by secret vote or by equivalent free voting procedures.

# Article 22

Everyone, as a member of society, has the right to social security and is entitled to realization, through national effort and international cooperation and in accordance with the organization and resources of each State, of the economic, social and cultural rights indispensable for his dignity and the free development of his personality.

Article **23**

## 1

Everyone has the right to work, to free choice of employment, to just and favourable conditions of work and to protection against unemployment.

## 2

Everyone, without any discrimination, has the right to equal pay for equal work.

## 3

Everyone who works has the right to just and favourable remuneration ensuring for himself and his family an existence worthy of human dignity, and supplemented, if necessary, by other means of social protection.

## 4

Everyone has the right to form and to join trade unions for the protection of his interests.

# Article 24

Everyone has the right to rest and leisure, including reasonable limitation of working hours and periodic holidays with pay.

# Article **25**

## 1

Everyone has the right to a standard of living adequate for the health and well-being of himself and of his family, including food, clothing, housing and medical care and necessary social services, and the right to security in the event of unemployment, sickness, disability, widowhood, old age or other lack of livelihood in circumstances beyond his control.

## 2

Motherhood and childhood are entitled to special care and assistance. All children, whether born in or out of wedlock, shall enjoy the same social protection.

Article **26**

## 1

Everyone has the right to education. Education shall be free, at least in the elementary and fundamental stages. Elementary education shall be compulsory. Technical and professional education shall be made generally available and higher education shall be equally accessible to all on the basis of merit.

## 2

Education shall be directed to the full development of the human personality and to the strengthening of respect for human rights and fundamental freedoms. It shall promote understanding, tolerance and friendship among all nations, racial or religious groups, and shall further the activities of the United Nations for the maintenance of peace.

## 3

Parents have a prior right to choose the kind of education that shall be given to their children.

Article **27**

## 1

Everyone has the right freely to participate in the cultural life of the community, to enjoy the arts and to share in scientific advancement and its benefits.

## 2

Everyone has the right to the protection of the moral and material interests resulting from any scientific, literary or artistic production of which he is the author.

Article **28**

Everyone is entitled to a social and international order in which the rights and freedoms set forth in this Declaration can be fully realized.

Article **29**

## 1

Everyone has duties to the community in which alone the free and full development of his personality is possible.

## 2

In the exercise of his rights and freedoms, everyone shall be subject only to such limitations as are determined by law solely for the purpose of securing due recognition and respect for the rights and freedoms of others and of meeting the just requirements of morality, public order and the general welfare in a democratic society.

## 3

These rights and freedoms may in no case be exercised contrary to the purposes and principles of the United Nations.

Article **30**

Nothing in this Declaration may be interpreted as implying for any State, group or person any right to engage in any activity or to perform any act aimed at the destruction of any of the rights and freedoms set forth herein.

This edition first published in 2021 by the Bodleian Library
Broad Street, Oxford OX1 3BG
www.bodleianshop.co.uk

ISBN: 978 1 85124 576 5

**Amal Clooney** is a human rights lawyer and humanitarian advocate.
**John Pinfold** was Rhodes House Librarian from 1993 to 2008. His most
recent book is *Petrograd 1917* (Bodleian Library Publishing).

Designed by Dot Little at the Bodleian Library in 10/14 DIN Alternate
Printed and bound by Livonia Print, Latvia, on 100gsm Munken Print vol 1.5

British Library Catalogue in Publishing Data
A CIP record of this publication is available from the British Library